AMY GRANT
THE CHRISTMAS COLLECTION

www.amygrant.com

Produced by
Alfred Music Publishing Co., Inc.
P.O. Box 10003
Van Nuys, CA 91410-0003
alfred.com

ISBN-10: 0-7390-7490-3
ISBN-13: 978-0-7390-7490-9

www.emicmg.com

Album Photography: Kristin Barlowe

A Note from Amy

Over the past 25 years I have written and recorded a lot of Christmas music, releasing new projects in 1983, 1992, 1999 and now 2008. Is there a limit to how much Christmas music one singer should produce? My children probably think so as they have been haunted for years by their mother's voice over holiday shopping mall and restaurant sound systems (part of my plan to not be left off their gift list). Personally, I never grow tired of Christmas music which compels me to record new songs whenever I get the chance.

For someone who grew up writing songs about life and faith, Christmas seems to be the one season when the whole world welcomes the Good News, the hope of peace on earth. That's why I keep making this music. In The Christmas Collection, I've chosen my favorite songs from my three earlier projects and added four new recordings. As always, I enjoyed being back in the studio with Brown Bannister, who is as easily moved to tears as I am by the creative process.

I'd like to thank all of the people who brought this music to life...the songwriters, musicians, singers, orchestrators, producers, engineers and to EMI for wanting to blow the dust off some of these old songs. Additionally, I'd like to thank my management company Blanton Harrell Cooke & Corzine and all the wonderful support staff.

Finally, I'd like to dedicate this album to Ronn Huff with deep appreciation for his brilliant orchestrations and his immeasurable influence on so many musicians. Ronn, you started me on this tradition of Christmas music and holiday performances. Thank you for inviting me to share your stage.

Contents

JINGLE BELLS

Words and Music by
JAMES PIERPONT
Arranged by
JACK GOLD and MARTY PAICH

Jingle Bells - 7 - 1

Verse 1:

8

Chorus:

Jin - gle bell, jin - gle bell, jin - gle all the way. Oh, what fun it is to ride in a

one - horse o - pen sleigh. Hey! Jin - gle bell, jin - gle bell, jin - gle all the way.

Oh, what fun it is to ride in a one - horse o - pen sleigh. 2. A

Waltz ♩ = 160

Verse 2:

day or two a - go, I thought I'd take a ride, and soon this

IT'S THE MOST WONDERFUL TIME OF THE YEAR

Words and Music by
EDDIE POLA and GEORGE WYLE

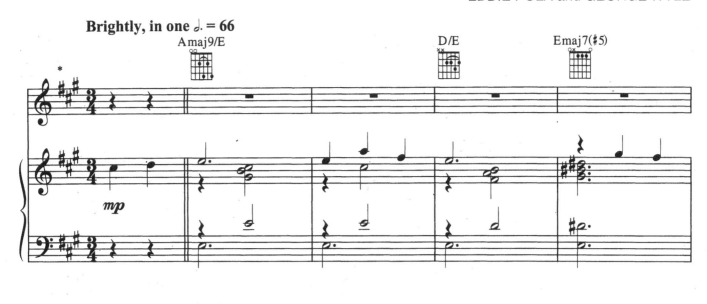

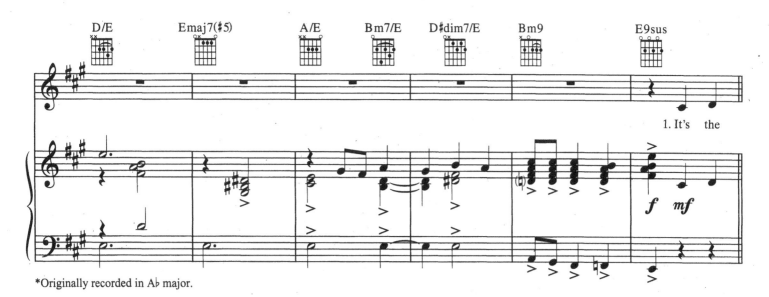

*Originally recorded in A♭ major.

It's the Most Wonderful Time of the Year - 7 - 1

14 *Verse 1:*

It's the Most Wonderful Time of the Year - 7 - 2

It's the Most Wonderful Time of the Year - 7 - 5

It's the Most Wonderful Time of the Year - 7 - 7

I NEED A SILENT NIGHT

Words and Music by
AMY GRANT and CHRIS EATON

I Need a Silent Night - 6 - 2

WINTER WONDERLAND

Words by
DICK SMITH

Music by
FELIX BERNARD

To Coda ⊕

BABY, IT'S CHRISTMAS

Words and Music by
AMY GRANT and VINCE GILL

*Originally recorded in F# major.

Baby, It's Christmas - 5 - 1

I'll al - ways give you _____ your fa - vor - ite _____ things. _____

straight 8ths

Ba - by, _____ it's Christ-mas; for you and for me.

(Guitar solo ad lib....

straight 8ths

SLEIGH RIDE

Words by
MITCHELL PARISH

Music by
LEROY ANDERSON

Just hear those sleigh bells jin-gl-ing, ring-ting-tin-gl-ing too. Come on, it's

Sleigh Ride - 10 - 1

Interlude:

love - ly weath-er for a sleigh ride to-geth-er with   you.
(Love - ly   weath-er for a   sleigh ride to-geth-er with

Love - ly   weath-er for a   sleigh ride to-geth-er with   you.
you.)

Repeat ad lib. and fade

(Love - ly   weath-er for a   sleigh ride to-geth - er with

you.)

COUNT YOUR BLESSINGS
(Instead of Sheep)

Words and Music by
IRVING BERLIN

BREATH OF HEAVEN (MARY'S SONG)

Words and Music by
AMY GRANT and CHRIS EATON

Slowly, with expression ♩ = 58

Breath of Heaven (Mary's Song) - 7 - 1

HARK! THE HERALD ANGELS SING

Traditional Hymn

Moderately fast ♩ = 120

Verse 1:

N.C.

1. Hark! the her - ald an - gels sing,___ "Glo - ry to the new - born King!

Peace on earth and mer - cy mild.___ God and sin - ners rec - on - ciled."

Joy - ful, all ye na - tions, rise,___ join the tri - umph of the skies.___

SILENT NIGHT

Words by
JOSEPH MOHR

Music by
FRANZ GRUBER

JOY TO THE WORLD / FOR UNTO US A CHILD IS BORN

Traditional Hymn
Arranged by RONN HUFF

Brightly, spirited ♩ = 104

70

TENNESSEE CHRISTMAS

Words and Music by
AMY GRANT and GARY CHAPMAN

74

GROWN-UP CHRISTMAS LIST

Words and Music by
DAVID FOSTER and
LINDA THOMPSON JENNER

78

Grown-Up Christmas List - 6 - 3

ROCKIN' AROUND THE CHRISTMAS TREE

Words and Music by
JOHNNY MARKS

1. Rock-in' a - round the Christ-mas tree at the Christ-mas par - ty hop.
2. (Inst. solo ad lib....

Mis - tle - toe hung where you can see ev - 'ry cou - ple tries to stop.
...end solo)

*Originally recorded in F# major.

Rockin' Around the Christmas Tree - 4 - 1

Rock - in' a - round___ the Christ - mas tree,___ have a hap - py hol - i - day.___

___ Ev - 'ry - one danc - ing mer - ri - ly___ in a

new old - fash - ioned way.___

Rockin' Around the Christmas Tree - 4 - 4

A CHRISTMAS TO REMEMBER

Words and Music by
AMY GRANT, BEVERLY DARNALL
and CHRIS EATON

A Christmas to Remember - 6 - 1

Verse:

A Christmas to Remember - 6 - 3

Light up the fire,__ play some Nat__ King Cole.__ Al-ways sen - ti - men-tal, and don't_ you know_ that it's_

__gon-na be a Christ - mas to re-mem - ber.__

2. I know it's

ber,__ to re - mem - ber.__

Guitar solo ad lib.:

To Coda

O COME ALL YE FAITHFUL

Traditional Hymn

Gently ♩ = 69

come, all ye faith - ful, joy - ful and tri - um - phant.___
Yea, Lord, we greet thee, born this hap - py morn - ing.___

O come, ye, O come,___ ye, to Beth - le - hem.
O Je - sus, to thee___ be all glo - ry giv'n.

*Originally recorded in B major.

O Come All Ye Faithful - 4 - 1

come_____ let__ us a - dore Him,_____

Christ_____ the

Lord._____

O Come All Ye Faithful - 4 - 4

HAVE YOURSELF A MERRY LITTLE CHRISTMAS

Words and Music by
HUGH MARTIN and
RALPH BLANE

Rubato, with feeling ♩ = 84

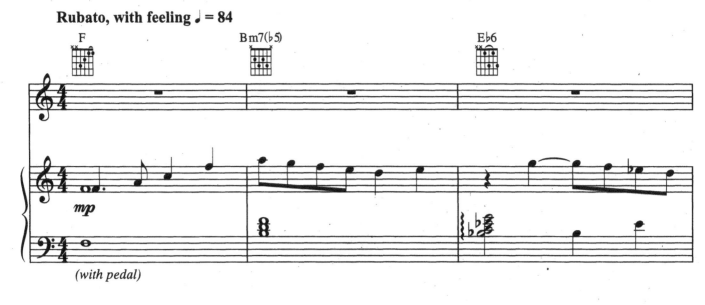

(with pedal)

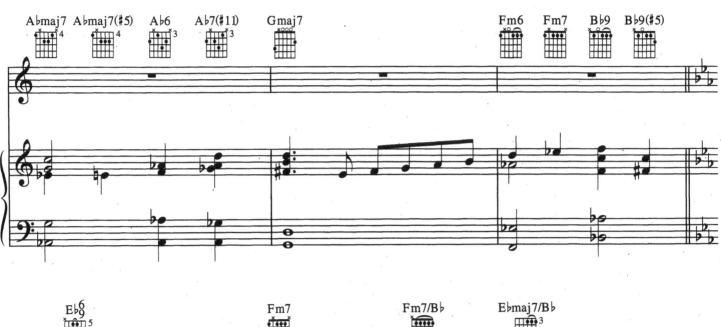

Have your-self a mer-ry___ lit-tle Christ-mas, let your heart be

Have Yourself a Merry Little Christmas - 4 - 1

98

A MIGHTY FORTRESS /
ANGELS WE HAVE HEARD ON HIGH

Traditional Hymn

Slowly and freely

Moderately fast ♩ = 132

Verse 1:

1. An - gels we have heard on high,_____

_____ sweet - ly sing - ing o'er the plains,_____

and the moun - tains____ in re - ply,_____

102

A Mighty Fortress / Angels We Have Heard on High - 5 - 3